Oranges: From Fruit to Juice

by Layne deMarin

Table of Contents

Drink Your Vitamins 2
Growing Oranges 4
Picking Oranges 8
Making Juice 12
Glossary 15
Index 16

Consultant:
Adria F. Klein, Ph.D.
California State University, San Bernardino

capstone
classroom

Heinemann Raintree • Red Brick Learning
division of Capstone

Drink Your Vitamins

Breakfast is the most important meal of the day. After sleeping all night, your body needs more fuel so you can get through the day. Orange juice is one healthy part of a good breakfast.

Orange juice is full of vitamins that keep your body healthy. It especially has a lot of vitamin C. Vitamin C is good for your body's blood, muscles, bones, and gums.

Growing Oranges

Orange juice comes from oranges, which grow on trees. Orange trees grow best in lots of sunshine, warm weather, and sandy soil. In the United States, most of the oranges come from Florida and California.

Orange trees stay green year round. They bloom in the spring with small white blossoms. In fact, Florida's state flower is the orange blossom.

Orange blossoms smell very sweet and attract bees. Bees land on the blossoms to collect **nectar**. They get some **pollen** on their bodies. Then they fly from flower to flower and spread the pollen around.

Pollen helps an orange blossom grow into an orange. It takes several months for a blossom to turn into an orange. During the summer the oranges are green. They don't change color until they are ready to be picked.

Picking Oranges

Farmers have to take care of the trees as the fruit grows. An orange crop can be damaged or even ruined if the weather gets too cold. Farmers also protect the trees from insects that want to eat the trees or the fruit.

Oranges are ready to be picked in the fall. Ripe oranges turn orange. Most of them have to be picked by hand. Workers climb ladders to reach the oranges in the trees. They fill large sacks as they pick the fruit.

When a sack is full, it is dumped into a large tub. When a tub is full, it can weigh as much as 900 pounds (408 kilograms). The only way to move these tubs is with a special kind of truck.

The special truck is called a "goat." It has a lift that picks up each tub. It carries the tub to a larger truck and dumps the oranges in there. When the larger truck is full of oranges, it can hold as much as 45,000 pounds (20,412 kilograms) of fruit.

Making Juice

The large truck takes the oranges off the farm to a processing plant. That's a kind of factory where the oranges are turned into juice. First the oranges are cleaned and sorted. Then a machine squeezes the juice out of them.

The juice usually has seeds and **pulp** in it, so it goes through a **filter**. The filter separates these bits from the juice. After that, the juice still has germs in it that could make people sick. The next step is to **pasteurize** the juice to kill any harmful germs.

The last step is to put the juice in a bottle or carton. It is sent to the store for you to buy and take home. Then you can drink a glass of orange juice for breakfast. It's a healthy way to start a new day!

Glossary

filter a screen that separates liquids from solids

nectar the sweet liquid inside a flower; bees make honey from nectar.

pasteurize to heat a liquid to a certain temperature in order to kill bacteria

pollen tiny grains of flowering plants that help the plant make seeds

pulp the soft, juicy part of a fruit

Index

bees, 6

blossoms, 5, 6, 7

cartons, 14

filter, 13

nectar, 6

orange trees, 4, 5, 8, 9

pasteurize, 13

pollen, 6, 7

processing plant, 12

pulp, 13

truck, 10, 11, 12

vitamin, 3